The Ghosts Call You Poor

andrew suknaski

the ghosts call you poor

macmillan of canada
toronto

ALGOMA COLLEGE LIBRARY

© Andrew Suknaski 1978

All rights reserved. The use of any part of this publication reproduced, transmitted in any form or by any means, electronic, mechanical, photocopying, recording, or otherwise, or stored in a retrieval system, without the prior consent of the publisher is an infringement of the copyright law.

Canadian Cataloguing in Publication Data

Suknaski, Andrew, 1942-
   The ghosts call you poor

Poems.
ISBN 0-7705-1656-4 pa.

I. Title.

PS8587.U55G85   C811'.5'4   C78-001041-8
PR9199.3.S873G85

Designed & produced at
Dreadnaught, Toronto

Printed in Canada for
The Macmillan Company of Canada
70 Bond Street, Toronto M5B 1X3

to john newlove
and george morrissette

Acknowledgements

Some of these poems have appeared or will appear in *Arts Manitoba*, *Boreal*, *CARFAC*, *Canadian Dimension*, *52 Pickup* (Dreadnaught), *Laomedon*, *Manitoban*, *Mr. Cogito* (U.S.A.), *Student*, *Descant*, *3¢ Pulp*, *Number One Northern* (Coteau Books).

"Mrs Krasniansky Mourning" and "Uncle Pillepko" appear in abbreviated forms in Myrna Kostash's *All of Baba's Children* (Hurtig).

The tenor and energy of some of these poems grows from sources found in the Alberta Provincial Museum and Archives, the Edmonton City Library, the Glenbow Archives, the Moose Jaw Library and Archives, the National Library and Archives (Ottawa), the Peter Whyte Library and Archives (Banff, Alberta), and the Saskatchewan Provincial Archives.

The author is deeply indebted to many people whose lives and shared knowledge were part of the beginning of this work: Bill Lee, Harvey Spak, and Dr. Günter Mende (of the Department of History at the University of Texas), who helped with information about Chinese history, migrations, and coolie labourers; the Reverend Father Oncescu and his wife Maria, Mr. and Mrs. Vasile Tonita, Lee and Marie Soparlo, and many others of Wood Mountain who related the disappearing oral history of early Rumanian settlers; George Auerbach and Dr. Jim Bartlett (from the University of Alabama) who helped with the metaphysical properties of ghosts and the elastic collision and hard spheres in a geography of open and closed systems.

The author thanks the Canada Council for an Arts Grant which provided some of the free time to complete this book.

The author is grateful for the invaluable critical suggestions of David Arnason and Ken Hughes at St. John's College, University of Manitoba.

Finally, the author is grateful to Dennis Lee for his continuing encouragement and editorial work on this selection, and to Charlotte Weiss, who finally shaped it, keeping the woman's heart in these poems.

Contents

Dance in Wood Mountain Community Hall 1
The Grave of an Unknown Homesteader 4
Smuts 5
Abandoned Métis Church 6
Dreaming of the Northwest Passage 7
Blood Red the Sun 11
Big Bear Speaking to Thomas Trueman Quinn 12
Mrs Gowanlock Remembering Duck Lake 13
Gabriel Dumont and an Indian Scout Changing Coats 14
Almighty Voice 16
The Indian and the White Man 18
The First People 20
Shugmanitou I 26
Shugmanitou II 28
Grass Fires 29
Jadah Zimmerman Recounting His Life 33
Dauphin's Peterson Bakery & Tea Room 35
Alexander Czornucha 36
Harry Grott 40
Retiring in Assiniboia 42
Birth of the Bull Calf 43
Finding a Home 45
The Grain Exchange 47
Uncle Pillepko 48
Union Hospital in Assiniboia 49
The Last Letter 52
Morning 53
Parting 53
What Keeps Us 54
Forgiving 56
Northern Light 58
Grizzly at Night 59
In Search of Părinti Dionese Necifur 60
Săt 65

Poem About Three Billy Tonitas 68
Koonohple 70
Mrs Krasniansky Mourning 73
Three Coffins Dream (circa 1850) 75
Stubborn Dragu Freezing To Death 77
Augusta nee Hoffman 78
Planting Potatoes 81
Capreol Red 83
Gunner Folgerberg 85
Bydwell's Well 87
The First Time 89
Love in the Manger 90
The Gold Mountain 91
Chinese Camp, Kamloops (circa 1883) 94
The Ghosts Call You Poor 96
Bienfait Cemetery, Thanksgiving 1975 98
Birnie 101
Betrayal of Earth 105
The Graveyard 107
Poem Written to Old Friends at Christmas Time 108
Letter to Harold Ogle 110
At the St Victor Petroglyph Site 114
Returning 117

*when the last red man shall have become a myth among the white men
. . . when your children's children think themselves alone in the field, the
store, upon the highway, or in the silence of the pathless woods, they
will not be alone.*
   Chief Seathl

*And on the prairie
the ghosts who own it continue to walk in clans,
searching for food and for what they once knew.*
   John Newlove

*well, andy . . . we'll see you again sometime.
the world is not so big we cannot
find ourselves again.*
   Bill Hanowski

Dance in Wood Mountain Community Hall

for bill and terry

it was spring
and i was home again
he sat down in a chair across from me and said
"you know
i've been watching you
i'm a poet too
and i've noticed even though you seem to be having a good time
nothing here has turned your crank... anyway
i thought i'd come and talk to you
i write poems about people too
i want to write one about you
but first i have to get an impression of you..."
for the first few seconds
we simply looked at one another
the silence heavy
the possible poem looming somewhere between us
like the scent of a fat pheasant in rosebushes
where two coyotes have arrived
both motionless and waiting
for the first sound
of crumpling leaves

he mentioned how
he'd been gazing out through the open door of the hall
and beyond... while i was watching the dancers
him thinking
that telephone pole out there
a fairly insignificant thing
but there are all those messages that leave this place
and arrive here... certainly a point of
entry into a poem
i didn't think it important to mention
all the telegraph poles a hundred yards north

2

had been hauled away years ago
nor did i bother to tell him the pole was actually a power pole
who cares for lies when glimmerings of possible truth
flood some dark recess of the mind?

we talked of the common friend who introduced us
i said
"our friend and i have a friend
he left those hills
fled to toronto and became a cbc camera man and producer
he got tired of bucking morning and evening traffic
along the don valley parkway
and later walked 5 miles to and from work every day
finally he did the near impossible
found an eastern city woman
who believes in gardens
and still has faith in family and the meaning of home
the last of her kind
in all those big places beyond...
anyway they married
and he came home to live on his late grandfather's farm
home to all the things he dreamed about
through difficult urban sleep
no...in my dream of failure
i thought this place was dying
but that was a lie
there is a light in nearly every house again
old friends return from their cities
and life continues here...
our friend's father once said to me
'this place will only die if we let it die'
i think he said that remembering his grandfather's
favourite rumanian proverb
if you plan on leaving your plough
your plough has already left you
a long time ago..."

2

what turns one's crank...as they say
what moves one?

i thought raking leaves in my yard
the day after the dance
...*the odd things that float*
through your mind
i once drank beer with a friend
and mused in my brief beer joy
ah how i love this friend his wife and their children
if by some strange fate he should die
i will marry his wife...take care of his children
and honour his memory
his death a year later
numbed me
with an odd guilt that grows each year

and this was turning my crank while the poet rancher
sat in the chair across from me
though i failed to tell him that
and when he left and the music began again
i walked directly to that late friend's wife
and danced with her for the first time in our lives

4 The Grave of an Unknown Homesteader

for brian coulter

walking the lonely stretch of railway track
from the abandoned lupick farm
i suddenly spot two pheasants
searching for tiny pebbles
on the edge of a very old grave

both suddenly rising
in swift flight
i shoot at the cock... miss
the hen falling
into cover
in the deep coulee
on the other side of the hill

search in vain
in the rosebushes
finding only the cold reproving wind
carrying an ancestral voice
beyond the meaning of name

Smuts

smuts... another prairie ghost town
how did a town with a name like that
ever stand a chance?
even if you could have said
"let's go for a beer in smuts"
imagine swallowing a line like
"yeh... lost my last two front teeth in smuts
was a dance
back inna thirties!"

smuts
every business place boarded up
every house abandoned
the only sign of life the
big ukrainian church
towering against a blue autumn sky
above the hill on the edge of town

smuts
sounding much like the ukrainian *skvarkeh*
"remains of boiled pig fat"
which at least is useful
mixed with liquid lard and a can of lye
to make soap

so why did smuts die?
who knows?
possibly the answer lies
somewhere between the overgrown riflepits north
and the small abandoned métis farms
strung out like a broken rosary
ending where the clearings widen
and other churches fade in the haze
all the way to alvena

Abandoned Métis Church

north of fish creek
and looming on the edge of yellow poplars
the church with métis gothic windows
seems the ghost of a failed dream

in the distant willows
the wind remembers in native dialect
visions of the nation
that might have flourished

across from the churchyard ending at the gridroad
métis children play among poplars
on the nearby farm
still unabandoned
like others along the road
where defeated men women and children
left for other places
the ancestral spirit crushed
by the undertow of the new
and by white men with money

Dreaming of the Northwest Passage

dreaming of the northwest passage
a polar ocean highway to the eastern world
and searching for an imaginary place to begin
some entry into the possible
taken by bearing straight from the point where
the longitude of the old
intersects the latitude of the new
that point
where the nebulous meaning of north
becomes the possible refuge
our first bronzed ancestor ambles to
season by season
sandia man
folsom man
the dorsets
thule
before commerce greed and all voyages begin

no dreaming of an ocean highway necessary
until the mohammedans bar
the way to india
until henry vii
gives john cabot and his three sons royal liberty
to sail unknown seas
john cabot circa 1467
bored with hugging coastlines
prefers the unknown
where the dream begins... the ocean highway
to the far east
the dream in later years young sebastian cabot carries
with him north one summer
where his terrified men mutiny
at the sight of monstrous masses of ice floating
in a land of neversetting sun

8

and so it all goes on
columbus and others
searching for the shorter and cheaper route
the expansion
the whalers seaming
a light of hope
while they pursue the greenland whale
keeping alive the dream
where death humbles men
till other explorers sail
...the expansion
moving toward eventual commerce
and exploitation by the civil man

the first esquimaux
captured
like a caged animal

the need to humiliate the native
beginning with those like sepulveda
the spanish theologian
and 16th century professor
firmly convinced indians were inferior to the spaniards
and therefore to be exploited...
or the unwavering conviction
of gonzolo fernandez de oviedo circa 1535
"indians are not far removed from the state of wild animals
therefore coercive measures must be taken
if they are to be christianized
and taught the uses of systematic labour..."

explorations
and a chronicle of ironies
leading to a single truth:
the native showed us the way
the native drew the first map on sand and earth
the northern esquimaux drew in snow
and did with small shale cairns
what contour lines do
to indicate mountains
for scottish and british explorers

the indian showed us the way to the heart
of the prairie
and distant mountains

2 arctic voyages

dreaming of passage northwest to the great sea far west
of a strait leading to it . . . the passage
the gentle esquimaux knew of
and tried to explain to the mariners

always dreaming of the passage
the scottish and british mariners
chose their ships' names well

hecla
        griper
                searchthrift
                              discovery
gabriel
        fury
                blossom
                          erebus
                                      terror

and you sail with them
on the vast sea within your ancestral sleep
till you dream of nothing
but men and ships battered and broken
by ice and wind
men burned by merciless northern sun till faces
swell and crack
bleeding
and you become obsessed
with the whole chronicle of obsessions
why we all dream
why we travel yearning for other things and places
and become obsessed with crippling fame
pride glory fortune and mariners' thirst
for knighthood
following the ultimate adventure beyond
to the northern sea

all ending in desperation
for franklin and his men shipwrecked
and far too proud to say
"stop! cease this madness!
we'll never find the way out of here...
best to learn survival
from the esquimaux
and wait
till others find us..."
and stories tell of captain penny a searcher on beechey island
finding the three graves of the first victims
of the fatal expedition overland
and how
it being summer
he discovered a small garden of arctic flowers in bloom
nearby
a pair of gloves hung out to dry
and somewhere between
a small fragment of paper reading "To be called..."

sir john franklin died on june 11th 1847
and all his crew was buried in the snow
only to be uncovered
by summer winds

erebus
        terror

crushed by gothic ice
and buried deep in the frozen darkness
northwest of the subterranean place
where it all began
the dream
myth

erebus... whence
nothing returns

Blood Red the Sun

blood red
the sun sinks to its knees on the edge
of the smoky plain
the pale moon grows older again
and the cree are told
they must learn to walk the white man's road
big bear's spirit is troubled
since returning from the northern hunt
he takes long lonely evening walks
and thinks of the great wheel of buffalo
no longer turning through the seasons
the sun grows heavy
and older
days become cooler while families grow hungrier
their clothes more worn
and ragged
the glow of women's faces
gone
like the light once mirrored by stones
no longer burnished
by the buffalo
shedding old fur
stars fade in the children's eyes
wandering spirit is speaking
"we come here to fort pitt
come for meat
we come for this thing *money*
we wish talk about these things
kapwatamut*..."

*kapwatamut: cree nickname for thomas trueman quinn,
trader at hbc post in fort pitt (1884).

12 Big Bear Speaking to Thomas Trueman Quinn

"we sign treaty with governor
he tole us we get meat
before payment...you heart stone"

big bear places hands flat
on own chest
then suddenly flings open hands
before quinn's face

"you want heart? here...take...
you need one!"

Mrs Gowanlock
Remembering Duck Lake

leaving delaney's home we were unaware
of what was about to happen
we had walked only a few paces
when the indians began to shoot us
when mr williscraft fell to his knees before us
i knew it was the end
a moment later my husband began to fall
his arms reaching out to embrace me
i caught him... and we fell together
i lay there frozen
with my face pressed next to his
he was taking his last breath
when an indian pulled me away
the indian dragged me through rosebushes
that tore my clothes and flesh
i was nearly crazed with grief and terror
later the indian women in some camp befriended me
i was cold and shivering
while they removed my shoes to dry them
they offered me something to eat
were very kind
and gave me a warm blanket
those women seemed a gentle morning one wakens to
from a horrible dream

14 Gabriel Dumont and an Indian Scout Changing Coats

for mick burrs

old antoine ferguson
born 1884 in st laurent saskatchewan
antoine remembering the old story
his father told before him
"there was this fog everywhere one morning
and gabriel dumont
he always use to get up early and go for hunt
but this time he went looking for horses
and all at once he heard this howling
something like a wolf
in those days there were wolves
but gabriel he realized this was no wolf howling
it was an indian
the indians they had this habit in those days
they signalled to each other
and they could understand
what they were saying..."

old antoine explains how dumont quietly ambled around
until in a clearing in the mist
he glimpsed the indian scout on a hill
dumont then slyly making a half circle
to ascend the hill
finally sneaking up behind the kneeling indian
the scout with cupped hands amplifying his message
while a knife lay at his feet
dumont seizing the knife
flinging it far into the mist
then swiftly grabbing the indian
one arm round his neck
old antoine explaining precisely
"...the indian really got scared
because he was positive gabriel would kill him
that was what *he* would have done..."

however gabriel assured the indian
"no... it is not our style or mine to kill
unless we have to
we don't kill for nothing...
but when you get back
you tell the others
'i met this man who had every chance to kill me
but let me go...' "
the indian replying
"nobody will believe me"

gabriel finally suggesting
"to prove it really happened
let's change coats... you take my coat
and say 'this man did that!' "
"no!" winced the startled indian
"they might shoot me
you know... another coat coming in!"
dumont laughed "no... they won't
not if you're alone"

and they changed coats
dumont murmuring
"by this jacket then
they will believe
it's *really* true
i could have killed you
but didn't..."

dumont
his own dreamer
and mythmaker

Almighty Voice

> LA RONGE, SASK.(CP)—
> A 3-year-old boy was killed yesterday
> by a pack of stray dogs. *The Globe and Mail*, Jan. 17, 1975

buying a midnight paper
from the shivering blind man
on bloor
i glanced at your sad story prairie child
walking home was numbed
to know your small body rose and fell
in the rapids of a mad dog pack
swimming the river of your blood one street length
to catch some bitch in heat

2 the wild dog pack

ghost of small prairie child
i sadly imagine your playmates
grown men and women someday
haunted by the futility of your death
when they discover the story
of almighty voice
beginning with the end
of buffalo
and the onset of indian hunger
almighty voice
78 years ago on one arrow reserve
shooting a treaty steer
for a wedding feast
to honour his indian bride
and father
old dust
only to be arrested and told in jest
that he must hang for the illegal act

the scent of blood
alerting the wild dog pack
howling for revenge
in the name of white justice
almighty voice escaping
to later shoot a policeman
then elusively running for 19 months
until the meaning of home lured him
back to the reserve
something in human nature
the waiting dog pack knew it could depend on
before chasing him further
to that famous poplar grove
in the minnechinis hills
to finally cut him down
in a niagara
of green leaves
and lead

small prairie child
almighty voice
the wild dog pack hunts us all
while we dream of those sweet fabled bitches
freedom
and justice

The Indian and the White Man

for shannon twofeathers

*the caribou do not linger over
the weak whom
the wolves cut down
we indians
we learn our laws of survival from nature
we do not mourn someone's death
any longer than four days
we do not keep a dead person's spirit
by prolonged mourning
but let it go free*

2

i am a white man
my father still lives
and yet already his ghost
possesses me
no less than other ghosts:
big bear
almighty voice
mrs gowanlock
riel
dumont
they all call us poor
and dwell inside us
often weeping for what is
and what might have been
in the broken circle of my memory
they clone daily
there are movements in the darkness
within willows and poplars
where winged things can be heard fleeing
while the forces advance

and i admit
i am a white man
and can be none other
can only say
"forgive us manitou... master
forgive us"

The First People

*to the memory of nelson small legs jr (23)
and eddie bazie (23)*

i genesis

unktehi made earth and all living things
insects birds animals people trees stones
forming the great vast "hoop" chane gleska

unktehi a feminine creator
gave birth to tunkan "stone god"
the oldest spirit of the earth
the powerful flint point floating up dreamlike
from cante ista "the eye of the heart"
to flood the first shaper's mind with an image
all leaning into hunger for lasting food
that might sustain the body and nagi "the spirit"
this
the hunkas "our first ancestors" of these plains
affirmed

takuskanska the "moving spirit"
wakinyan "thunder spirit"
tunkan
unktehi the "water spirit"
gods tangled in the manes of the earth's four winds
when the first hunka gripping a crude stone
scratched a cross on a mammoth's shoulder blade to honour them
a cross
hunkas' first sign

chane gleska the sioux's sacred hoop
binding all things and gods into one
"the great mystery" wakan tanka "the great spirit"
later to become manitou
meaning not only the great spirit
but also "the prairie"

a sacred place alive with sound
furred and feathered things filling the vast hunka memory
the dream of ikche wichasha "the first people"

ii the first people

the first people of the plains were humble
knew they were not worthy enough
to speak directly to manitou
and therefore appealed in prayer or song
to intermediators:
winddriven takuskanska
wakinyan a vein of fire slashing the black wrist of night
wakinyanpi "the winged one" soaring the high winds with all
that has come free and true

iii prayer

sing a wankan olowan to wi
"a litany honouring the sun" flooding with warmth
the crucible of the fertile earth
pray to shugmanitou for endurance
he weaving your dreams of feather and bone
held in a geography of glistening teeth
the scentful wind shuttles to looming manitou
but pray

pray to shoonkawaka of the plains
"holy wild horse" and bloodbrother to coyote
pray for courage
that your herbal dream of freedom and home be mapped
by hunka gods listening and held true
to hoofprint coördinates on water's
soft sandy edge

pray with care to the good sister ookjekeehaw
"magpie" robed in formal black and white
and hope she grant you generosity

pray to wizened uncle khaahxree
"crow" the returning sun's faithful blacksmith
forging north in the bellows of renewed spring
to give you new strength

that your dream float high above the black anvil
of death

pray to tunkashila wamblee "grandfather eagle" for wisdom
pray as the young sioux boy prayed to become a man
through the four day fast
ending with his first holy vision

"tunkashila
              tunkashila
                            tunkashila
grandfather... grandfather spirit... help me!"

pray as even the starving baby's lips moved
in a muted litany against the sioux mother's frozen nipple
when the first blizzard arrived at wounded knee

"tacko eena
              tacko eena
                         tacko eena
mamma... mamma
i'm hungry"

pray this way to wi and hanwi "the sun and the moon"
who watch over manitou
and who are the eyes of eternity
held in the fateful geography of common blood out there where
your life begins
pray...

"maka tanhan wichasa wan 'i am one of the earth'
hunka grandfather spirits keep me
only the earth endures
only the earth endures
tunkashila wakan tanka
tacko eena
             tacko eena
                          the spirit is...
hungry"

iv failure

peacefully resigned
and dreaming the white angel of freedom leading your people
the broken hoop made *one* again
you said nelson small legs
"bury me in these hills back of the house
so i can look over the land i fought for..."
and was it like black elk's vision
of the six hunka grandfathers and a voice speaking
the first grandfather telling of power
the thunder beings bestow on the worthy
a power lifting one to the earth's lonely centre
to see things as they truly are
or the fourth grandfather
promising power from the earth's four quarters
to help you walk and reach the centre of the nation's circle
and take "a cane to walk with and a people's heart
and by your powers... make it blossom"?
ghosts of the past looming
and battles
a voice finally saying
"now you shall walk the black road with these things
heavy in your heart... and as you walk
all nations with roots shall fear you"

you left three notes nelson
written in a thin delicate hand
one to the people
one to the loved ones the relatives
and the last
to the leaders of the movement
"farewell..." you said
"take care... i will always help you guys
from the other side"
that other side being something more real and lasting
not "the green frog skin world" of money lenders
they wasicun "the fattakers" bloated on the blood
of the first people
become a community of placeless ghosts

lost in the avenues of ancestral blood
wasicun "the white man" betrayer
of the first people

  v the ascent

  the shaman's dark god whispering
  "climb...climb that high hill
  back of the house your father built"
  gaze to the high blue mountains beyond
  where the ancients always said
  one's strength would come
  pray
  pray to shugmanitou
  hope for the soothing voice
  of some grandfather spirit
  try to sleep
  and like the old indian women say
  "*you pray*
  pray on that high holy hill
  and what you see
  what you dream
  will...come true"
  and when the sad wail of shugmanitou
  draws you from fading margins of sleep
  and you know there's no going on
  prayer having failed...descend
  descend
  descend to the deep valley
  where the river swells
  growing colder

  vi descent

  unktehi's soft compassionate voice counselling
  "when the river rises
  and the current threatens
  to pull you
  to your knees
  stand
  for all
  who must follow..."

life is not so easy
as a walk across autumn prairie stubble
to that place
where the dark coulee begins
one ought to remain
endure if possible
and if not
what better way
than the muted colours of 23 autumns
mirrored on the edge
of a bronzed bullet
to brighten the dark centre
of one *last* dream?

nelson small legs...if God
were human
and could suffer the way
the sky once suffered
he would not have sent his son
but would have done it himself
long ago
to spare you
and us
this pain

Shugmanitou I

for james wounded horse

slowly climbing the high hill on the reserve
all the way to the top
glimpsing shugmanitou* at the edge of
wounded horse's grave
where two straw bales
still remain
shugmanitou's thin shadow cast
across the fresh earth
while he watches
for eetoonkhallah†
stirring
in the sweet oat straw

2

james
ole pinsetting buddy
and master poolshark
who in my youth taught me
the laws of elastic collisions
and hard spheres... forgive me master
for not being here
the day they honoured you
forgive me master
teacher of my first sioux word... "manitou"

3

finding the bright flower wreath
the war veterans honoured him with that day
where the wind has carried it

*shugmanitou: coyote in dakota
†eetoonkhallah: mouse in dakota

to the cemetery edge
i return to set it back
on his fresh grave
and with a dry willow stick in hand
ask myself
"where shall i lay the wreath
and plant the willow
to keep it here?
by his head?
or across his heart
where my shadow now falls? no...
better plant it at his feet"

only the sound of eetoonkhallah
this windless day
and shugmanitou watching
watching
from a higher
hill

sioux indian cemetery/wood mountain
spring 1976

Shugmanitou II

"i tellya *boy*
them skidoos's kind
compared to that strychnine
they useta use
i rode across my pasture one winter
an saw where a coyote fell an took a fit about
thirty times before he died from the stuff
wen i finally caught up to him
he was still kickin his last pattern in the snow
like them there snowangels
the kids make

"hell *boy*
them skidoos's much kinder
you jus chase onna them coyotes
till is lungs burst
then you *stop*
right on toppa im
yeh count to seven
one
       two
              three
                     four
                           five
                               six
                                     seven
then yeh drive away
he'll never move an inch"

Grass Fires

a great purple and grey plume
the smoke arcs high into evening sky
the arrowshaped lot burns
while village men lean on rakes
black silhouettes against the low blood red sun
remembering old loves
a parked model-a beyond the last elevator
beer and love
following some dance night

they slowly gather to reminisce about old grass fires
the one that swept though someone's homestead
east of elm spring
and how it burned the shack and all possessions
while the family watched from the straw barn
or the year the big one
rode the mane of a north wind from ferland
down to glasgow montana
and in recent years
the one lightning began
on the edge of burnt thigh's grave at the reserve
and how it crept north to the village
they recall the wind tiring that day
finally yielding to desperate men

the old rake
in my blackened hands
i lean into gathering dusk and silence
gaze at the old men gazing far beyond the dark side of memory
where small smouldering fires between the indians
halfbreeds and others
have dwindled
into a single spark buried forever with old james wounded horse
sixteen war veterans ambling
beside the flag draped coffin

carried by six halfbreeds and indians
to the sioux indian cemetery on a high hill
early this spring

2

with my rake
i carry the fire along the edge of lovenzanna's coulee
and on to the tall dry grass bordering
the rumanian cemetery
in a short while
the whole pasture is burning to the edge of the schoolyard
where the ghost of my boyhood sleeps
in a small coulee
and i remember how i hid the last bottle
of my mother's chokecherry wine there
before the principal strapped me

here in the faded grass
burns the baseball that was
my only homerun
here smolders the last mystery
the last memory
three drunk halfbreeds hungering for easy money
in a dark alley behind the pub
that thirties night
here smokes the damp rotting two by four
its crude spike
rusted the colour of dry blood
and the witnessing wind
no longer cares for questions like
"who *held* the two by four that night?
and how much money
did the old timer *have*
on him?"

here on the cemetery edge
the wind changes
and the fire burns on toward nameless leaning crosses
another man
is running to help me beat it out

we finally smother it where the last cross reads "*alex
hominuk*"

3

and here
in the dry chloroformed grass of my boyhood
sinks the memory of all these
unspeakable things
into new meaning
where another voice is softly clearing its throat
to reproach the sentencing man
who is also me
"they paid for what they did
and one had the guts to stay and
become an altar boy
kneeling in the pain of guilt forgetting
and shame
married and built a home
later humiliated by the big fat girl
who hung his two small daughters
by their belts on coathooks
in the cloakroom
following an argument
'i *may* be an indian
but i am *not*
a murderer!' "

4

and you out there will say
"ah ...
he's still yammering about the same things
the same gloomy crap
even tainting it with racism"

but i tell you
some things were what they were
are what they are
and you do not bury truth the
way a dog
hides a bone

you have all travelled far too far
for me
and all too fast

i no longer care to arrive
too soon
where you are
but take the advice of a young woman
who once said to me
while i burned in my yearning for other women
and things called new territory
"stick around a while longer sweetheart
there's territory here you haven't even begun
to discover..."

Jadah Zimmerman Recounting His Life While Gallagher Listens

can't remember exactly now
when i came to this northern city
but here i am
in this dark corner here in the mayfair
opening to closing time
drinking this yellow rat piss
but let me tell you kid
i once had my chances too
wrote poems
things weren't so easy then
ah yes... women so fine
they turned my knees to putty
and i often thought the first time
i met each one
my blood was a sack of sand
flung at my heart
once was this fairhaired woman
with skin like velvet
breasts firm as new mushrooms
just after a rain
well i tell you kid
i turned my heart inside out for her
was like a hat driven by the wind
against a telephone pole
but she's gone long ago
like the rest
all of them like a tad of thyme
in my memory
stale as day old mashed potatoes
yes kid... she was so beautiful
my mouth went dry
the first time i saw her
and what hurt most
was when she left

i turned to two dollar whores to forget
but only remembered her
more and more
yes it was a long way down
anyway it all ended
when this lovely cree girl
took me to her place
when she opened this green battered door
scarred with knife marks
her old withered mother rolled out in a wheelchair
and creaked down the hallway
to the fire escape
well i said to that young girl
"forget it princess
here's twenty
bring your mother back
get yourselves a better place to call home
find a job if you can
this is no life for you"
well kid
she stood there with tears in her eyes
and i left that day
the end of that trip
forever
and that's when i turned to rat piss
but what does it all matter now kid?
here i am

Dauphin's Peterson Bakery & Tea Room

in the peterson bakery & tea room
even the scarred benches resembling church pews
remember the smell of soya sauce
when some thin chinese still ran the victory cafe
and you wonder why he ever sold the place
but now only older ukrainian pensioners
gather there each day to exchange the local news
over a cup of strong coffee
and you watch one of them with a bear paw hand
gently tugging the sleeve of
another's green army and navy parka
impatiently patiently waiting for a story to end
while still another small man
savours a slice of freshly buttered bread
slowly and meditatively dunked into his cup
to further sweeten in the wellsugared coffee

and you know each day must be the same
old men waiting to remember their last stories
till there's nothing else left to tell
when the full peace is attained
and you watch them braiding and unbraiding
their workenlarged hands
ominous with arthritic joints
where flesh has swollen like leavened bread

gazing at these proud widowed men
you wonder how many wives overworked to reach an early grave
or if the intoxicating aroma of fresh bread
nudges a single man's dream
toward that immutable memory of home

Alexander Czornucha

> *"when the russians moved into the ukraine*
> *i told my brothers in the carpathians*
> *'all you have left now*
> *are the songs you sing' "*
>
> andrew suknaski, sr.

retired ukrainian farmers of the valley
make home
the towers hotel
at the end of dauphin's mainstreet
and alexander czornucha "the dark one" crowding 90
is among them
and only God knows how alexander
fully fluent in french latin german and four slavonic languages
world war one veteran
and once a professor somewhere in the austro-hungarian empire
ever wound up as a manitoba farmer
slowly shattering his body with 40 years of discered stones
halfdeafening him
and still ringing in his ears
whenever he cares to remember warm summer sun
high over riding mountain

in the towers hotel men 20 years younger than alexander
reverently call him "geedo" or "colonel"
and when he reminisces about the old world
one of them listens and nods relentlessly
"yah yah...yah...yah"
the sad truth being that no one
no one ever understands a thing
beyond faint glimmerings
alexander's ukrainian pitted with polish russian and german
and only during saturday morning wrestling on tv in the lobby

do they perfectly understand him
his curses narrating the action
"dgeetko... abbeh yeeho shlock trafogh
... whoolehrrah!"

2

when the middleaged waitress gives me my coffee
i ask her about alexander
"oh ole geedo... he comes downstairs about 11 each morning
has the same thing every day
a plate of chips and gravy at supper time...
why don't you go up and talk to him?
room 223 at the far end of the hallway"

after coffee i go upstairs
alexander opens the door a modest crack
and eyes me suspiciously
after the first few difficult words
he welcomes me and seats me on his huge black coat
his second blanket on the bed of the cold room
i note the flyswatter hanging behind a framed print
of a painting of a young lady in a long white flowing gown
to the right of the single window facing the late noon sun
alexander sits on a worn wooden chair
his glasses thick as a magnifying glass mirroring the sun
while he talks
and it isn't long before alexander's soliloquy pulses
with a heated rhythm
"we ukrainian... we are good gentle people
we were *never* aggressors
we defended ourselves against the vikings
tartars turks magyars russians poles and swedes..."
he waxes on about stalin and russia
"a man must have humanity
without humanity a man is nothing
he becomes an animal... stalin
was such an animal
oh yes... it didn't take them long to russify the ukraine
and they talk of the black sea
for us... it was always the 'blue sea'
and so it will remain
always..."

and as alexander's vast vision of history unfolds
i too like the others
keep politely smiling and uttering
"yah... yah yah... yah"
and it is only a vague slavic feeling about the cadences
that draws us closer and closer
while i occasionally wedge another question into the silences
to launch him on still another fiery tangent

after several hours alexander talks of two lost wives
"the first one
she and i were together for seven years
in the end she became ill and finally passed away
and i buried her in garland
the other one... i buried her 23 years ago here in dauphin
and i still remember it
there i was on that last farm in the late fall
and i thought to myself
'the snow is falling... and i am alone
the water is boiling in the kettle on the stove
and i am alone...'
so i said to myself
'to hell with it... may as well sell the place
and go to town...'
so here i am"

the light in the room is fading
and alexander's dark eyes visible now grow darker
while i imagine an even darker sea beyond them
where graceful viking ships are sailing west
and i tell alexander i have to catch a bus
we both rise him towering above me
and his hand is a vise of flesh and bone
while we shake hands him saying
"gripping someone's hand like this
this has always been my way
ever since i was a small boy
when my father put me on a horse
that day a terror seized my heart
and thinking i would fall
i held the saddle horn as if i would never let go
and i've always shaken hands this way ever since

yesterday a friend and i went to the coffee shop
down the street... he slipped on some ice
and falling it looked as if he would crack his head
like a coconut on the concrete
well i grabbed him by his thin arms and he cried out
'alexander... let me go you're hurting me
alexander... where does your strength come from?'
i told him it was the faith and humanity inside me
and the way it has grown
through the years in this valley... that power
and i assure you son
if there were no humanity in you
i could crush your hand
holding you here forever
if i wanted it so..."

Harry Grott

stacy balon dauphin valley pensioner
never drinks more than one glass of beer a day
here at the towers pub
and when he gets up to excuse himself
his story follows him and what i think might have been a poem
leaving me with one dubious racist line
muttered in ukrainian
when four young wood cree from pelican rapids
sat down at the table next to us
"yah neh loobloo yeah... tee chornee
cohsh yeeh toot nahsrahloo...
'i don't care for them those black ones
something has shat them here' "
and i think to myself
"*oh well... you are what you are stacy balon
a sour jaded man...* "
and just then harry grott seated beside me
turns to me and says
"you are a white man
you white men speak of a god who walks and talks
we cree... we say God is the earth we walk on
the water we drink and the air we breathe...
what you say white man?"
at this point i'm still thinking about stacy balon
that cynical bastard
and almost speak out loud
"*too bad you never learned to speak english stacy
and learned a reverence for beer
you would still have been here and you might have
learned something about your 'black ones' *"
i snap out of my beer dream
and begin to speak to harry grott
we talk about the great spirit

and i agree with him
we white men came with strange ideas to this prairie

i order harry his friends and myself another beer
and he tells me he was two years old
when his father took him to the grandfather's place
"i was 15 when it dawned on me
there was something funny goin on
my brothers and sisters was always comin to visit me
so i asked my grandmother why i was livin with them
my grandmother was a good woman
and she told me the truth...
that's when i knew my father and mother didn't love me
so i run away from my grandparents' place"

harry tells how his grandfather told him many stories
and i ask him to tell me his favourite
his black eyes brighten as he remembers
"the sioux...they come to fight us wood cree one time
the cree was cookin some food this night on an island
in this small river...they saw the sioux
on this horizon when the sun was settin
the ole women they said
'we too ole now...we stay keep fire goin
rest you sneak way on other side the island
we stay here till mornin when sioux come...'
the sioux come and found jus the ole women
they jus left them there to starve an die
they call that place now 'sioux river'
i bin there myself...big fish there
funny sound sometime there at night"

it's closing time
and harry finding out i'm ukrainian
asks me to say something to him in my language
"teh dohbrah leudinah harry..." i tell him
" 'you're a fine person harry' "
harry nods and smiles then replies in wood cree
"what does it mean?" i ask him

"you okay youself...white man"
and we both laugh

42 Retiring in Assiniboia

"i got a $50,000 house there on 3rd avenue
my wife passed away
and i'm alone now
it's a big lonely place now
didn't seem so big
when she was still here...
there are too many memories
come three o'clock
i gotta get out of there
i can't stand it
i come here to the franklin
have a few beer...
my kids
i hardly hear from them any more
they never phone... love?
i'll show them love!
i still got the farm
i'll sell it... onna these days then
that son and daughter in law
they can go live somewhere else
for themselves...
they think i drink too much
maybe i do
but it's my money
my years of work
my loneliness...
three months they never phone me now
never sent a christmas card...
have another beer!
i buy... come on
have a beer!"

Birth of the Bull Calf

for terry and cameron

being born
it falls into light
and the soft straw bedded stall

the young man says
"it's dead..."
his older friend kneels by the bull calf
presses his hand
against the delicate ribcage
"NO...BY GOD IT'S ALIVE!
that was a heart beat"

he jumps to his feet
picks up the calf by the hind legs
and shakes
a white fluid draining
from the small mouth
lays the calf down
and kneeling again
clears the nostrils
covers one with one hand
and mouth to nostril
face to face
gently breathes into the small expanding lungs
his young friend
pressing on the small rib cage
the other man
filling again with breath
the calf's lungs
both men working
in perfect rhythm
till the older man
sees the bull calf's eyes move

feels a breath
against his own face
finally he says
"born dead...
but alive now"

he and the black bull calf
rising at the same time
in the day's new sun
flooding the barn
with bright light

Finding a Home

father
my work can no longer keep up to you
your endurance defies myth
and your life will not be made a scarecrow jingle
i mean there you were
that early winter of 74
bushed
and resting in the assiniboia general hospital
saying "...i took the greyhound last night from lethbridge
a few days ago
i overheard your sister saying to your mother
just once in my life
just once
i wanna beat the shit outta him
like he's never bin beaten before
it had come to that
i knew then it was time to leave
that chinaman and your sister
they were fools trying to get your mom and me
together again
anyway
why should i die there among those indians in alberta?
i come back here to die
it may be all rumanians
but i know them
and they're my own people"

2 sharegardening

now you are well again father
and flourishing in an old widow's spacious home
in your 87th year
you claim to have finally found love
some say you've been seen walking with your new lady

hand in hand
to the post office

i have to praise you father
spading up this woman's whole backyard
to plant a garden you proudly show me
while we walk to still another widow's backyard
across the alley
where you've been *sharegardening*
as you call it
and growing five pound potatoes

3 the fire

last fall
smelling smoke
in your peaceful afternoon sleep in the easy chair
you did right father
immediately calling the fire department

after they rescued your lady's voluminous breast
from the washer wringer
the fanbelt finally stopped smoking
and the story spread like a prairie fire
till in a single week
you became a legend in the whole south country

what can i say?
except that when the news reached wood mountain
mother was slightly jealous
and is reported to have said
"now you have to be a pretty silly woman
to get your breast caught in a wringer"

well father
what can i say?
i guess there is hope for me yet

The Grain Exchange

uncle tom in '29
a lonely single man getting his kicks
playing the grain exchange in moose jaw
dreaming of becoming a millionaire
betting $3000
the day of the crash

the news of the crash landed like a pile driver
in the middle of his heart
he paid his rent for one more month in the rooming house
bought a can of lye with the remaining change
mixed it with a bottle of pilsner
and downed it

they pumped out his stomach
and my father visiting him in the hospital that day
asked
"why did you do it?"
uncle tom rationalized with some pain
"you got a wife and family
and land
money was all i had
there was nothing left to lose"

uncle tom died three days later
his thin arms knotted
in his groin

and i often wonder
if his ghost ever returned to the rooming house
to enjoy that last month
of free rent

Uncle Pillepko

uncle pillepko
arriving each spring with still another
case of pilsner beer
to celebrate the yearly visit
and reminisce with father about uncle tom
always wondering *why?*

i remember standing in uncle pillepko's lap
and savouring the first taste of beer
carefully studying the label
remembering the picture then
it seems there are fewer indians and
rabbits on the new label

remembering uncle pillepko
the old railroad worker
how his solid thighs beneath my child's feet
felt like wood
and maybe the way the corral post
must have felt
beneath his aging feet that spring morning
while he tied a baling wire
around his neck
and jumped
to swing from a crossbar
above the stockyard gate

Union Hospital in Assiniboia

in the latest photograph father
wearing the rumpled green suitjacket you were married in
you are seated under a small window
beyond the top of your illuminated head
a tuft of grizzled hair arcs
like a flame
snug in the upper left jacket pocket
the metal christ glows on the dark wooden crucifix
and a bone white hanging cord
curves down over christ's wrist

yes father
i have written some dubious poems about you
and said what i wished
but the stern pride emanating from the darkness
surrounding your hawk's eyes
refutes it all
as if to declare
"say what you want poet
but here i am
the living testament and icon
the survivor..."

2

easter sunday father
i walk to your lady's house on 7th avenue
neither you nor she are there
like a common burglar i peer through a window
to be *spooked* by the deserted room
and a barren table
then note the backyard garden
not dug up
"maybe they've already moved to the pioneer lodge"

i walk a few more blocks to the lodge
and check the name board
nothing
finally i phone the hospital from a gas station
"yes...he is here"

arriving at room 112
i find your faithful lady seated beside you
and holding your hand
your face and arms whiter than an empty page
at the end of a bible
your eyes glazed
"XHRISTOS VOOSKRAS" i say
wishing you happy easter
"vohyeestoo noo...vooskras" you respond
ponderously adding
"pahn yehzus...veet martvegh...stahw
veet marvegh...stahw"
'christ has risen from the dead'
the words fading
into a half whisper
your lady tells me you've been here a week now
and this is your sixth time this winter

you speak much slower now
finding it important to tell one more story
"hominuk...heez tie horrses von time by house
dhey stendin dhere all nite
peeplee say 'by jimminy...dhat hominuk
heez be qvite dha farrmer
heez be ploughink all nite' "

visiting hours over
your lady rises
and gives you one brief kiss
i too say goodbye...kissing you on the forehead
and slowly walk your lady home
she taking many rests
and always saying
"oh andy...he's bin good to me
i've done my best
i've tried..."

near home
"i wore this dress for him today
it's the first time i've wore it
made it from the cloth he bought for me
for my birthday...oh andy
he's bin so good to me
the nurses say he'll be out in a few days"

3

love is a bright flowered dress
when you are 60
and walk seven blocks a day
to and from the hospital
to see your 88 year old man
your first man
found beyond the margins of hope

love is small short steps with flowering pain
under spring blue sky and sun
of another 28 celsius day
knowing tomorrow it will begin again
you finally leaving the hospital
asking the usual
"how's he doing?"
the nurses walking in twos or threes
replying so softly
"fine...just fine..."
then chuckling to themselves
you murmuring again
"...guess he'll be able to come home
in a few more days?"
a young one reassuring you
"yes...just a few more days"

The Last Letter

for lianne

in your last letter you ask
"how are you?"
i still stubbornly smoke my pipe
though it's suicidal in my condition
i've grown a moustache and full beard
wear glasses now
and no longer comb my hair funny
but part it letting it fall sideways
knowing there's nothing left to hide

sometimes i'm still cruel
to those who love me most
even though i've grown gentler
i can still bring the toughest woman to her knees
beyond the tears where she lives
and i am not proud of this sickness
"nothing hurts more than a kind man
who's turned cruel"
said my new love one evening
seated in a dark alcove where she cried
while the rain fell on a distant street

sometimes a small animal
still leaves its hutch in my brain
to burrow on the lower edge of my ribcage
four years after you
i've learned to say
"i love you..." to another woman
but the stars do not dance
when i speak

Morning

remembering your bright smile
those mornings
when we first loved
and it was all
so good

but i have become this winged dark thing
beating a frozen sea of ice
in its last circle

so hard
not to choke
on the bitter taste in my mouth
that once held your sweetness deep
on my morning tongue

Parting

there are women whose leaving
hurts so much
it alters the taste of food
meals are left only partly eaten
if you are a fisherman
times become so difficult
you lose interest
in fishing
and throw back all your catch
on less fortunate evenings
the trout steal all your worms
leaving you with nothing
but an empty hook

What Keeps Us

"what keeps us?" i asked an eastern woman once
"i don't know...but tell me
if you ever find out" she said
and she is gone now

"actually"
wrote the paternal astrophysicist
recalling a love of his distant youth
"i've had an experience like yours
it gave me three sleepless nights
but my recovery powers have been excellent
that was 20 years ago..."

what keeps the white ptarmigan and her mate
in the high tundra mountain winter
on the frozen edge
of a juniper bush
silent in the memory of summer?
who knows...who knows what ever keeps us?

what kept the old ukrainian jew
arriving 40 years later
at edmonton international airport
his baba nervous on the observation platform
her flat chest and granite nipples
taunting the wind with joy?

"it is the first touch we remember
like a stolen apple"
a young woman may say
to the ghost of her lost love
while her firstborn sleeps in the late afternoon

"it is the last memory of the first time
cradled in the corner of one good uncataracted eye
enjoying another summer
though the body begins to hurt as the dark clouds arrive
something like that"
says the grateful old timer at medicine tree manor
in high river alberta

what keeps us?
"fear..." say the old
deserted by friends
ghosts feeding pigeons in the deadend street
just around the bend
up from the children's pool... fear keeps us
makes us settle for less

what keeps us?
"if i knew..." thinks the failed poet turned grocer
"i wouldn't be polishing hard green apples
i'd be running that florist shop across the tracks
where welldressed men buy roses
to make fragrant their betrayals..."

i told that eastern woman
"i believe in nothing i can touch
only in things that last forever
your warmth that bridges our sleeping bodies
and the early morning light along the edge of your face
i will remember if you should leave some day
will keep faith
believing there is still one woman
as fine as you..."

every douglas fir tree falls some day
and turns to earth
mountains slowly wash to the sea...
i believe only in things lasting
forever

Forgiving

there was that mountain summer
and then you returned to your eastern city
and unlike proud oldworld men
who believe a man must never follow a woman
i followed you

and now that you're gone
i wonder how you
ever stood it

me
a man too much alone
along margins of endless
people
and looming failure

you were tough sweetheart
tough and far more precious
than you may have known

i praise you
for lasting as long as you did
with a plainsman
far too sick
with this western hate

2

do you remember
when we drove your lonely nana home
that christmas eve
how we kissed her good night
in her small ontario town
next to the river?

i loved her no less
than the great grandmother i never knew
and who was struck dead
by a runaway team and wagon
in a polish village street
exactly 133 years ago
today

3

i only wish you the best now
all the finest things
arms of more merciful men
and finally some man
deserving
whose daughter
will not be calling me
father

the ghosts call me poor
and a fool

Northern Light

learning to face love again
and arriving
at the end of all this
very tired
our heads pillowed on one another's thighs
here . . . she and i fought like mountain lions
she demanding the plywood be removed
from the north window that
i said faced into nothing
i see our ghosts
still lingering by the chimney
where i nearly struck her in my rage
but she is gone now
beneath this world
you and i hold between us
has become all women i dreamed of beyond our cries
and the brief loneliness descending each time
they say she shares a farm
does things with her hands
she swore she'd never do
and grows in the boundaries
of another man's love . . .
now there is you
your youth
and all you've taught me
for you i took down the plywood
so you could hang the blue curtain
for you
this northern light
to trace my aging face
along your thighs

Grizzly at Night

may
one month before the indian paintbrush flourishes
the mist descends the cold mountain

hands deeply pocketed
i walk home from a friend's place
a fresh loaf of bread
warm against my chest

a grizzly looms up from dark deadwoods ahead of me
stops
and shakes the frost from his mane
then looking my way sniffs a sweet aroma
nods his voluminous head
as if to say
"what are you carrying so carefully
beneath your coat
pilgrim?"

remembering her gentle white hands
braiding the bread
i silently answer
"something to keep me warm brother
warm against the cold
this side of the river"

In Search of
Părinti Dionese Necifur

for years the stone walls three feet thick have stood there
the windows gone
wooden rafters and roof gone
the man of that place gone
and though i often passed the stone house
and was moved by its lonely beauty
looming in the evening light on that hill
i never once thought of what kind of man once lived there
whether he lived alone
or grew in the boundaries of a woman's care
and the love of children

i was young and only *my* life mattered then
the stone walls were merely something
casting a long morning shadow on summer days
when i helped vasile tonita and his sons
haul hay bales from the slough one mile northwest of
st peter and paul church on the correction line
the massive windows of the stone house
were only a frame for the distant descending sun
as we returned to wood mountain

and when i grew up and moved deeper into the margins
of what i thought it meant to become a man
i left home for what seemed a more meaningful world

having grown older
i return to begin again
hoping to reclaim the lost

*părinti: rumanian for parent or father; ecclesiastical address
for priest, or for monk acting as priest; respectful address

2

părinti... i've listened to the old men and women
who gave their best years
to change these hills into home
and enough to keep their young
heard those who've listened to the stories
over and over again
and yet so little drifts from their memory into light
so little is known about you still
who you really were
and what finally became of you
returning home to rumania

părinti... you seem only a myth and ghost now
a ghost still secretly measuring with a string
a best friend's shadow behind his back
or was it your grandfather's shadow?
you părinti that young monk saying to himself
"dear God... forgive this one last transgression
this honouring of the old
and ancestral memory of who i am... this string
binding me to all these mysterious things
i take with me to the new land
to bury in the wall of a house
a fortress i will build of stone to shelter the spirit
something that will stand indomitable
forever... like my grandfather
a ghost leaning into wind
walking home from the stony fields of his youth"

they say you came from constanta... părinti
your ancestors roman merchants and war veterans
who grew to love the blue sky of high summer
while they savoured their wine in open air tavernas
and told stories chronicling struggles
on the edge of the black sea
the text confirming your liturgy was tempered with latin
though the myths of your land were slavic
and most important
the belief in the soul's power
so much so that for centuries

a child was always sacrificed and buried
in the first wall of a new home in the old country
something later replaced by the measuring of someone's shadow
it being the extension of the soul
and if someone saw you
he or she feared death would come
in forty days

ah pǎrinti we poets are such dreamers
forgive me for this fantasy
... you were a simple man
they say you came to our prairie
and built a house from stones your parishioners gathered
from their fields
a monument to their hard work
and a place where they could bring their children
to be baptized
you planted a maple down from the hill
where your house still stands overlooking everything
and the tree growing taller than anything in these hills
casts a shadow across the west wall
when the late evening sun is low
and days begin to lengthen

3 spring 1977

pǎrinti... standing here by your greening maple
i am a boy once again in all my willow green dreams
for the man that has become me
and part of all these intangible things
keeps returning to a story told
by your friend reverend father oncescu
"yes sir yes sir i can tell you sir
pǎrinti dionese necifur
he built that stone house... i remember it
he came in 1910 in november
i know him perfectly
he stayed with john stefan
then 1911 he purchased homestead and preëmption
there where the stone house is
he had a dugout in the ground a couple years
1911 they started to build the church

they brought lumber from moose jaw
oh quite a few they went with the oxen
so they brought the lumber
and fulla by the name nicholi john zoara
that mean 'star' in rumanian
he paid for the lumber
he paid for all the icons
they brought icons from jerusalem
and in 1913 was ready

and it happened to be i came here and visit
1913 in february and i help them
i wasn't priest that time
but i helped them to do some church service
so everything was in order
people was coming people was coming to church
but he dionese lived in a village for one winter
was priest at st peter and paul church
1928 dionese was in car accident
lost his memory
in a little time he went back to rumania
before he left he was robbed here in village
was given bum cheque full payment for farm
they got him drunk and fooled him
then in regina was robbed $2,200
two rumanians rolled him
took his life savings
he was given some money by rumanian friends
and went back to constanta rumania... sad"

părinti... i am still a dreamer
and somewhere in the lupick coulee near wood mountain
long before my time
there are still no decent roads
someone poor and thin with a love for walking
someone known as părinti
is being carried on the back of a young rumanian
fording a swollen stream in the spring
and in the village
people are waiting for the wedding that will take place
... and memory being what it is
i do not know if it is you părinti dionese

or the now blind reverend father oncescu 87
whose faithful maria known as 'darkness' in hebrew
is his light
a young girl
the way he remembers her
when he could still see
the places you also walked... părinti

Săt

"om vinit din săt wood mountain post
'i came from the village wood mountain post' "
they would say to someone inquiring
or "om vinit din săt moose jaw"
they remembered as they left the prairie
their creaking wagons and whinnying horses
resounding through the hills
where they were told they would find their homesteads
and a new home

"om vinit din săt..." murmured the faint ancestral faces
peopling the memory of the old home
these men and women knew

with wagons and horses
they carried their supplies south
from moose jaw
the journey taking five days
till they arrived on the northwest side
of twelve mile lake
it was may and growing warmer
while they camped
and explored the country for four days
till they all agreed
on what would be known as săt
"village... or settlement"

they built sod houses with brush and sod roofs
and lived together for two years
till surrounding land was surveyed
and became available for homesteading

there were seven families that year of 1906
and their names were:

yordaci adamache
costantine mehiau
john stefan
dragu cojocar
angil cojocar
nita cojocar
john stoian
george chiro
badar tonita

2

vasile tonita remembering what his parents told him
"the first few years
the nwmp checked the people once a month
to see that all was well
and that there was enough food and fuel...
the police from the old post gave a permit to săt for $2
to cut some wood up in the wood mountain hills
it was said that wherever they unloaded the wood
that was where they would get their homesteads
but they dumped it all in one place at săt
so it didn't quite work that way...
before they all homesteaded
the government gave them authority to break some land
they sowed about 20 acres of oats
they bought a ripper somewhere
and cut the oats and raked it into piles...
the fall of 1907 at harvest time
the men worked on threshing crews around regina and dysart
pitched bundles for $1 a day
a day and a half of work meant 100 pounds of flour
anyway they made enough money to buy supplies in moose jaw
for a second winter"

mrs vasile tonita remembering what her parents
the adamaches told her
"my mom and dad went to dysart with a team and wagon
in the spring of 1907
they led back a cow and calf
it was a two week journey...
they also brought four or five chickens

when they were coming home
they say everyone was there at the edge of săt
they were all so happy
they had milk cheese butter and eggs for the rest of their stay
in the winter they played cards a lot
visited one another and told stories
about the old country"

vasile's final words
"and i guess it was lonely sometimes
waiting... you know
waiting for land
of their own..."

3

new year's day 1977 and two miles beyond flintoft
riding in the warm truck with lee and marie soparlo
marie the daughter of vasile tonita
a silence broken when lee points across bright yellow stubble
above glaring white snow
"you see that single tree just beyond
mind
where the snowfence has fallen...
just to the right of the tree
and by the crick in that bit of coulee
down from the railway track... that's
where săt used to be..."

Poem About Three Billy Tonitas

for al purdy

blacksmiths horses teamsters all are gone...
except one last teamster
vasile tonita
you will always see him heading up wood mountain's mainstreet
in winter if you're a regular
at 9 a.m. coffee in the store
vasile's team nearly half his age pulling a sleigh
loaded with seven bales of sweet oats
for his cattle in the south pasture
near the rumanian cemetery
if you're still there with the old men in the spring
you will witness one of the team become
vasile's spirited saddle horse
as he returns down mainstreet
from checking for newborn calves

on hot summer days
while vasile is out in some southern pasture
fixing fence with his old rubbertired wagon and team
a lone hawk circling the blue sky of vasile's thoughts
will often bisect the white vapour trail of a 747
young nephew billy tonita pilots from vancouver to toronto

later on autumn days
when study becomes too difficult for vasile's grandson billy
still tired from his assiniboia paper route the night before
jet streams high beyond school windows
may become harnesses pulled by a cloudwhite team
the whole earth a house
like the shack his two grandfathers vasile and naugu tonita
hitched their teams to during threshing time
at the end of the thirties
to pull it quietly off a cellar stash of homebrew
while the stingy old farmer

guarding the cellar door
snored peacefully through his noonday nap
the pure cold and amber brew
enjoyed thoroughly by everyone
before they returned to the field chuckling
and joyful

Koonohple

for myrna kostash

mother enjoying some tea
and remembering how they grew koonohple back in galicia
tells of baba karasinski planting the precious round seeds
in the spring
and how she later coddled the young green leaves
the male and female plants growing side by side
from a single seed
baba wanting only the best always weeded out the male
so the female could grow tall and strong
there was never any difficulty telling them apart
though the male plants grew first
the females always flourished taller in the end
"why bother with the runts" baba must have thought
"they're only like some geedo...an obedient shadow of baba"
she probably assumed that in one's garden at least
things could be perfect
and anyway it was the female who bore all the seeds
she could survive alone

when the crop was ready
baba and geedo would harvest it with sickles
and tie small bundles
later buried in a muddy trench near a creek
where they were left to rot for one week before being dug up
and taken to the creek to rinse
finally koonohple were hung on a fence to dry
and a few days later geedo battered them with a flail
till only the strong hemp thread within the stalks remained
then baba's final delicate work began
using a huge piece of circular wood with many spikes
she would comb and comb the threads
until they became almost as fine as gossamer
then on winter nights baba and other women

got together with their bundles of combed koonohple
to tell stories while they spun by hand
spun every bundle into fine thread wound onto big wooden spools
they called "vahrahtmoos"
and mother says
their arms and hands were their spinning wheels
the thread was dyed with beet plum or carrot juice
and woven into cloth becoming
table cloths towels curtains
and clothes for a whole family

fascinated i ask mother
"what did you do with the seeds leaves and stems
after you flailed koonohple?"
mother sipping her sweet tea slowly remembers
"vee kept seeds fhorr nex yearr
an throw strrah to dha peegz...
dhey vaz shure like dhat sthoff"
i ask if she grew koonohple on the farm
she smiles
"shomtimes... ohnly leedly bit fhorr burds
i gif dhem seeds in veenterr
oh dhey shurr like dhem... sing soh nice"
she tells how in the old country
geedo used to press oil from koonohple seeds
and she wistfully recalls how good it was on salads
a bit of chopped homegrown onion and sliced cucumber
a tad of pepper and salt
"smell soh ghoot... dhat oil
vit leedly veenyeegerr
nhoting else now *soh* ghood"

smiling i ask mother
"you know what koonohple are mom?"
as she eyes me suspiciously
i tell her
"grass mom 'trahvah' that's the stuff the kids smoke mom"
she lifts her braided fingers high above her head
rolls her eyes heavenward
and exclaims
"oooh my God... marryyohnah! dhat's be marryyohnah?"

and now that i mention to mother
how the kids often grow their own hiding it with corn stalks
she slowly remembers how her father
grew his illegal tobacco at the turn of the century
and hid it at the centre of his koonohple crop
that always grew taller all around
she remembers that when the first world war came
tobacco was scarce everywhere in the old country
and geedos suffering withdrawal beat their babas
the old women scuttling to neighbours everywhere
to beg for a bit of tobacco
geedos tried bulrushes and nettles and simply anything
and mother recalls how her grandfather silent as granite
in his corner of the living room
was often lost in a cloud of rising smoke
like a chimney on a cold windless winter morning
baba coughing and chiding geedo
"dgeetko...vahryatstvo!
ahbeh tehbeh shlock trahfogh!"
geedo always mumbling between well spaced blissful eternities
and keeping his secret
"fynoo baba...fynoo...fchoh budeh yak zohlotoh
'beautiful old woman
beautiful...everything will be like gold' "

Mrs Krasniansky Mourning

a whole year now
sharing her house with another widow
her hurt and loss become a slow forgetting
and over strong tea with her new friend
she remembers more and more of the past
a time on the prairies
when it was suicidal to reveal one subscribed to *pravda*
more often now she remembers the good times
and her husband
a faithful old country communist
receiving his bundle of papers at the local post office
every two weeks
remembers him reading proletarian truth
and burying it in the farmyard
out of fear

she remembers the end of the second world war
their poverty
and need for something better to call home
remembers how she and her husband
and two small children
protested outside the regina legislature
she still treasures the faded news photograph:
the four of them
smileless
each with the right arm proudly flexed
with a fist
tightly formed
the ultimate pride

they scoffed at religion and God
yet recently digging through his old things
she found the hidden litany
he wrote giving thanks to the virgin mary

after the new house was built
she copies it over and over again
imitating his spidery slavic calligraphy
and learns to write in her 70th year

she curses him less now
and recently with thin arthritic arms forming right angles
is known to have said
"if he could only be here now
i would carry him on my arms
like this"
her widow friend understanding the need for some humour
in all this slavic mourning
said
"might be he get heavy *baba**"

*baba: grandmother in ukrainian

Three Coffins Dream (circa 1850)

julia suknaski remembering

great grandfather domich woke up one morning
from a haunting dream
dali might have turned into a painting
and fortune

great grandfather domich
vividly recollected the dream for his wife
"in the house in the village where my brother lives
i saw three coffins levitating
in the middle of the living room
...a door opened by itself
and one by one
each coffin floated out and up into the sky
and they flew away like wild geese..."

great grandmother domich consoled him
"think nothing of it...it's only a dream"
but he saddled his horse
and left for his brother's village
when he arrived the door was slightly open
as he entered the house he gasped
his brother and the wife were lying dead
then looking towards the bed on the indoor oven
he saw the dead hired girl
suddenly
he heard a faint cry
from under the covers on his son's bed
lifting the edge of the quilt
he saw the baby suckling its mother's breast
great grandfather took a blanket and wrapped the baby
cradling it in his arms
he mounted the horse
returning home that day
to build three wooden coffins
that was the year cholera swept the country

he sadly told great grandmother domich
"dreams... you are right
don't believe in them
'they're only dreams...'
this is all that remains
of ours"

Stubborn Dragu
Freezing to Death

1906 a heavy snowfall that winter
young george soparlo homesteading by the first coulee
beyond shanley hill
made a note in his diary
"heavy snowfall...
creeks overflowing their edges this spring"
one final may blizzard was moving down from the northwest
when dragu finished his morning coffee
in his friend soparlo's sod house
dragu mentioned he was on his way to cut some firewood
in a poplar stand west of them
soparlo going by an inkling in his bones suggested
"it don't look good... dragu
i wouldn't go if i were you"
stubborn dragu disagreed
being certain it wouldn't amount to much

he left soparlo's house and walked over to his own place
at the edge of the sheltering thornapple grove
he picked up his axe
and headed out across the tall grass above the snow
after the storm lasting for several days
dragu was found frozen far east of the poplars
7 miles from the hoffman place
where the family lost two daughters in the same storm

george soparlo found the remains of a small fire
dragu managed to get going to warm himself
soparlo often wondered if his friend
ever heard the bell mare with the roan stallion team
the hoffman girls went looking for
and never brought home

Augusta née Hoffman

augusta née hoffman born 1892 in power north dakota
writes her story the family story for some local history book
she begins
"this won't be easy for me to write
and should anyone try to read it later on
that won't be easy either
as what reading and writing i do
i had to figure it all out for myself"

five years without a crop
her father joins a railroad gang in the mountains in montana
his wife and five children later following him there
in the spring of 1903 they all leave for wood mountain
travel with a covered wagon and faithful team of horses
a saddle pony six head of cattle and $600

she continues
"we children walked most of the way
and the country was alive with antelope
seemingly they could not understand our wagon
and would circle around it over and over again
when they got too close we would get inside
on our fourth night's camp
a man with a team wagon and dog 'shep' pulled up
not too far away
we went over to get acquainted
but he said very little
nothing of where he came from or where he was going
we kids fixed that we called him 'neighbourhood'
he never went too far away
but also never offered to be friendly"

the tenth day and nearing wood mountain
they pass a buffalo skull with a rock wedged in its mouth

and finally settle near the spot where santee lodges once stood
near the wood mountain post
that winter becomes the worst ever seen
trees are broken by the weight of snow
one time the cattle get away and the father and mother
go searching on foot
by nightfall when the mother isn't back
the father lights a lantern
and then crosses a creek and climbs a high hill where he calls
holding the lantern high over his head
he does this till midnight when he hears his wife call back
augusta remembers
"she had come across the buffalo head with the rock in its mouth
while it was still light enough to see
she stopped and collected her thoughts
as to what way she should follow the dim trail
and from there made her way home..."

for money in order to survive
they put up hay and haul coal and wood
for the northwest mounted police
the mother makes butter for the police
and washes their clothes
the family is happy
until the tragedy occurs
"may of that year will never be forgotten
as one of the worst sorrows of my life took place then
i was the one that did all the riding
to look after the horses and cattle
that spring dad esther and i left for glasgow montana
and that would take us seven or eight days
on our last day when we were fourteen miles from home
we woke up to find a cold rain falling
after going five or six miles
we met walter on horseback
he told us ruth and nellie had gone the evening before
to get the horses and didn't come back
he had been out all night looking for them
but the wind had gotten so strong
and the rain had turned to sleet
one of the horses wore a bell
but you could neither hear or see anything...

we hurried home as fast as the team could make it
the first thing was to feed the horses
then tell the police
they went down east and let those people know
and the few people who were there turned out for the search
after three days it began to clear
but we knew they couldn't be found alive...
after a week's time
dad and walter took a tent food and wagon
and camped down one of the poplar creeks
about eight miles from home and searched every coulee
they found the team of horses
and kept looking till every foot of ground was covered
not until eight years later
were the remains found two miles beyond where
the folks gave up looking
mother picked up every little bone
and thanked God for letting her have even that much
she took them and buried them
in the end of the garden..."

Planting Potatoes

for the kierans

remembering once again that easter journey
through the green and gentle
rolling mountains of the kootenay older mountains
where the greed for gold ran its course
mountains where people have more at stake
and more human than the young rockies
bright sun in the blue sky
and crossing kootenay lake on the *anscomb*
to drive west from balfour where the old men were fishing
by the abandoned pilings
where steam boats no longer stop
saying to my friends
"when i went back to school 15 years ago
i lived with a family
a few miles up ahead
and i have this feeling
can tell you exactly what we'll be seeing shortly
the beautiful old man
will be in his garden
just down from the apple trees
where the young daughter her brother and i used to stand
waiting for the school bus
and he will be planting apples
his hair will be snow white"

remembering the first and second turn
before the road straightens
by their postbox
and my friends were suddenly speechless at the sight
a white haired man planting potatoes
in the rich black earth
and much thinner than i expected
"stop..." i said then

"i must say hello to him
it's been many years"

and it all returns to me now
like the slow slow growth of potatoes
the gathering memory of those cold winter mornings
how he rose long before us kids
often hearing him along the margins of sleep
the old house creaking quietly
as he walked to the kitchen and woodshed beyond
me often waking to sounds of splitting wood
he used to light the stove
and later waking again with
"hots boys! coffee's ready!"
then he would gently murmur to his aging wife the schoolteacher
"time to get up sweetheart..."

i can still taste those pancakes
potato pancakes that sustained me and stuck to my ribs
like a swallow's nest
clinging to a rafter
and something of the stories he told on sunday afternoons
to the nelson doctor and his wife
still clings and grows
inside me... stories always beginning
"now when the mrs and me were still living down in the hat..."
or "when we moved to macleod..."

i could almost give away my right eye
just to eat
one more of his potato pancakes

1975 toronto/1976 wood mountain

Capreol Red

having a coffee with a man who rode freights
in the thirties
he telling me how he and his friends
wore striped railway hats so railway policemen
couldn't tell hoboes apart from the brakemen
he remembers capreol red a cnr bull
who became a legend in the thirties
he loved to terrorize men sleeping
at the edge of the railyard in capreol ontario
red's favourite trick was to sneak up with his german shepherd
and let the dog snap at a sleeping man's neck and ears
other times he'd enjoy the mile ride
out of capreol
walking on top a moving freight
red would sneak up on some man climbing the iron ladder
between two boxcars...at the last rung
he would crush his victim's fingers with one foot
as the man fell to the singing rails below

no one knows how many men fell this way
before the young negro boy from winnipeg
laid low one night on a boxcar as a freight left capreol
when red finally came along
the boy emptied a pistol into the bull's body
my new friend says
"they found capreol red and the pistol
by the 18th telegraph pole
one railway mile out of capreol...
nothing was ever said or done
and that boy is an older man now
enjoying his daily beer in some winnipeg pub
where he often tells the story
i have the odd cool one with him
whenever we run into one another in the pub..."

then he adds
"yep... capreol red
they say when the son of a bitch was killed
things started to get better across the whole country"

Gunnar Folgerberg

lee soparlo speaking

"now gunnar folgerberg was a
real morale booster
he bet becky justice one time
he could jump over 7 chairs
he said *becky...*
you line up 7 chairs
n all go over there n take off ma shoes
n jump over them
they were both drunker than skunks
an everyone here in the west central
laughed like hell
well the boys lined up 7 chairs
an gunnar
he walked over to the end of em
unlaced his shoes
an placed them gingerly
in front of his feet
an then jumped over the shoes
well sir
he an becky justice argued like hell
gunnar saying again an again
i said
you line up 7 chairs
n all go over there n take off ma shoes
n jump over them
n i done jus that
anyway
gunnar won his bet
it was a case of 24 beer
which they drank together
after the bar closed"

2 thirties dances

"in the thirties when they had all those dances
you'd always see gunnar there
drunk an amusing people
he had no teeth
an ee had this comical way of keeping time
with the band
he'd tap his feet
an slap his thighs an hands
an every once in a while
he'd touch his mouth lightly
an make it pop
lotta guys tried to imitate em
but they never could
see they all had teeth
an couldn quite do it like gunnar"

3 the mine

"gunnar operated a mine
mined lignite coal
south of bill lethbridge's place
actually just 2 or 3 miles
southwest of maxworth

there was a fulla called fieldberg
worked for him
drank like hell
like gunnar
they say fieldberg came home one night
sat down at his table to
have a nightcap
and fell asleep on the table
tipped the coal oil lamp over
with his head
i guess the table caught on fire
and he burned to death

yeh ole gunnar
they use ta say in the thirties
*gunnar keeps the people warm
an happy*"

Bydwell's Well

driving home south from assiniboia
lee soparlo tells another story
"mind . . . you know where the sidoricks used to live
well john elbow
lived just a lil north of there
up that gridroad that makes a jog in the coulee
you know where those big poplars grow

anyway john elbow was a bugger for drink
christ
drink all night
wake up nex morning
lookin jus like a wet moccasin stretched over a fencepost
but ee'd be right back there at your farm the next morning
diggin another well
we never had cribbing in those days
he use to line the walls with stones
nicest job you ever saw
would last forever

heard im joking one time in the west central
said
wen i die
i wanna be buried face down
so all my enemies can kiss my ass
was a real card
onna those rumanians half gypsy half turk

one time ee came ome pissed good and proper
went to the well to get some water for a bean soup
well ee boiled her up
was eatin away wen ee bit into some bone
said to himself
goddamn . . . never put any meat in 'ere
well he checked a bit closer

and found the head of a gopher
and talked about it in the west central all through the thirties

    he dug one once for bydwell up ahead here
    got down about 60 70 feet
    an ee hit this big blue stone
    bout a foot an a half in diameter
    right in the centre of where he was diggin
    anyway he punched a hole in the stone
    with a crowbar
    well they say the water shot straight up clear to the top
    they say as john elbow was climbing the rope
    the water was right at his backside
    helpin im up...

    that's the place right over there
    where bydwell lived
    he's dead now
    the well was just east of that big poplar
    was onna those artesian wells
    there's a big slough there now... jup
    bydwell's well"

The First Time

"i remember my first time
we were overseas
me and freddie
we both met at the same bridge
in a small german town
he was carrying a sack of cabbage
he'd stolen somewhere
and i was carrying a sack of potatoes
that's how we paid for it then in the army
it was the first time for both of us
you know it wasn't sordid
the way it is now with those kind
then you were sort of helpin out
keeping some family goin
anyway freddie an i tried to describe it the next day
in the messhall
he said it was like being on the end of a
good solid punch
that sends you clear through a bay window
without a scratch
i said
it felt like a thousand sparrows
flyin outta my asshole
all at once"

Love in the Manger

i was still a boy at those dances
in the town hall in the early 50's
when i overheard her whisper to her lady friend
while their children slept on a wooden bench
"them thirties was not always so bad
i remember a barn dance my husband and i went to once
we was lovers then
the bright red geranium waltz was playin in the loft
i was a virgin
and we was in the manger...
i remember nothin sweeter now
my right leg was around his waist
and the left over the edge of the manger
i can still feel the breath of his whinnying horse
on my thigh
when we came
and it was lovely"

The Gold Mountain

"who asked you to be born poor...?"
the looming ghosts always whispered
to the chinese coolies
working for 7¢ a day
in a crowded twang tung province
till the good news arrived
a lush and mountainous
promised land in the east
...a glimmering of hope
"THE GOLD MOUNTAIN"
canada
where each day was another $1

and leaving canton or hong kong
for the gold mountain
a coolie was led to believe
five years' work on the new railroad
would mean $300 saved
enough to buy freedom
land
and room to breathe fresh air
back in the homeland

on arrival
the coolie found the rules were already made
contracts stipulating
"buy your oil and rice in the company store
or else..."
the storekeeping gougers inflating prices daily
as the coolies' expense list grew
"pay for company tools
or else...
pay the revenue and road tax
or else...

pay for religious fees
or else..."
pay for doctors and drugs
or else..."
and the coolies paid and paid
saving here
and there
till scurvy took its toll
till the long workless winters sapped savings
to nothing
until the dream grew tired
of the cold
and its chattering teeth
a profound and measureless loneliness
nudging it along backalleys
in search of one
frozen potato
and possible warmth

the dream
and most of those who dreamed it
are gone
only ferns and forest flourish
where they once pitched their tents
and smiled
for the rare photographer

and on the southwestern edge
of the gold mountain
spring avalanches and rains
carry bones from shallow graves
down to the great river
flowing to the sea
the last trace of the coolies' dream
a genetic memory forever locked
in a knucklebone
on some pacific beach
and like a sea shell held to an ear
something very old speaks in the language
of unimaginable silence

something steeped in the whole earth's pain
wedged between stone
and the bonecrushing breakers of the sea
"the ghosts call you poor...the ghosts call
you poor..."

Chinese Camp, Kamloops (circa 1883)

in the photograph he stands alone
under a willow
before the small tent
the shadows are long
likely an evening in early july
his left foot is extended slightly
beyond the other
on the edge of his shadow
at the base of the tree
two washbasins lean perfectly
against one another
like two coins in a child's hand
his clothes are baggy
his arms are flexed
you would like to be romantic
and believe he is reading
a letter from his parents back home
or a letter from some young lady
he possibly dreaming of her small delicate hands
tiny feet
and body smooth and soft as silk
exactly the way it was supposed to be
if your family were rich
and you were a girl
growing skilful at some craft
you constantly sitting
to ease the pain from tiedup feet
knowing the suitors and matchmakers
would always ask
"let see feet... how small?"
the oriental myth
the smaller the feet
the softer the body
but no... if this young man had a sweetheart
she was likely poor

and walked to work
like the rest of the family
simply surviving
her feet growing naturally...
looking closer at the photograph
you become realistic
and realize...no
there are no letters for this lonely man
he is only rolling
a cigarette

2

in the second photograph
his two friends
standing ten feet apart
actually pose:
one smiling
and revealing
a missing tooth
...the other
an unusually tall man
looking
almost stately
a stern face
that might have been
the face of an emperor
behind them
a simple table
and two stools
in the shade
of a tree

3

by the third photograph
oriental clothes have been worn out
it's likely another summer
the men are wearing cowboy hats
and pointed riding boots
the new clothes fit more snugly
across angular bodies seeming thinner
and solid
as anvils

The Ghosts Call You Poor

for the bill lees

"who asked you to be born poor?"
the old saying
the coolies brought from the orient
remembering it
                on fevered nights
                till it became

...*the ghosts call you poor*

when one was ill
the opium steeped dream tapped
                its meaning in ancient code
                in the mind
tapped like chopsticks in an arthritic hand
trying to pick up

the last rice grains...from a bowl

the coolies
           familiar names

   lee   kwon   ching   and hoy

nostalgic men
their lovers abandoned
                men victimized by *bak kuei*
                "white ghost"
                the white man

                men who befriended *yin chin*
                "the indian"
                sharing their degradation

bak kuei . . . ignorant
                   of the common truth

we have all suffered
to build this country

                "the ghosts call us
                . . . poor"

Bienfait Cemetery, Thanksgiving 1975

three cree horsemen ride high over a single sun
engraved on roche percée
where a tall hoodoo wall slowly crumbles
into the souris river unemployed miners fished
during the summers so long ago

and i am walking east up railway avenue to the crossing
am trying to imagine that indian summer day
of october 4th 1931
600 men and women silently shuffling heavy feet on gravel
the women carrying their boundup babies
the young and old men four abreast
and everone crying
while 18 veterans carry three black caskets
laden with bright fresh flowers
a funeral procession that began at union hall
and ended at the common grave

54 years and nine days later i am a stranger walking alone
only the sound of my own feet on the same road
am troubled by last night's ghostly thoughts
where i stood before the ukrainian church at the end
of main street
imagining some grandmother inside
down on her knees the sunday before it all happened
and the demonstration turned into a riot
a goya nightmare... some grandmother ending her prayer
with one treasured memory of her late husband
the way he could will away the most foreboding premonition
with a single favourite adage... some grandmother
remembering their only son
down in the mine
"fynoo baba... fynoo... fcho boodeh yak zohlotoh
'wonderful grandmother... wonderful
all will be like gold' "

walking down this quiet road
my thoughts turn to mrs budris
whom i talked to only a few hours ago
mrs budris widowed twice now
"my name was markunas then...
my husband and i had only been married for two years
he was lithuanian
i wasn't in estevan when the riot took place
i was at home in the village at the mine
with many of the other women
we all heard about it that day of course
my husband was shot in the stomach
the doctor wouldn't admit him to the hospital in estevan
he said
'nobody gets inside this hospital
unless there's a payment one week in advance'
so some miners drove my husband 50 miles to weyburn
where he died a few days later...
no more
dreams of better working conditions and a union
the men were all very scared
and went back to work without a word...
yes... it was a long time ago
what is to be said about it now... who cares?
but it *did* happen"

arriving at the common grave in the cemetery's southeast corner
i stand by the undated head stone of *baby konopski*
and read the stone of the three miners

        LEST WE FORGET
          MURDERED
    ESTEVAN Sept. 29, 1931
        BY _____

P. MARKUNAS
   AGE 28
         N. NARGAN
           AGE 28
                J. GRYSHKO
                  AGE 29
    IN MEMORY OF
DISTRICT MINERS #7606

and i remember once again mrs budris
saying how THE R.C.M.P. was later chiselled away
and the word MURDERED filled in
at the same time when deep bullet marks on the head stone
were covered by a thin layer of fresh concrete

as i leave the grave site
a large southbound truck slowly lumbers past
i glimpse three men in the cab as they look my way
while three mallards rise from the slough
next to the crossroads

heavy grey clouds drift east
the only sound is the dry rustle of cattails nearby
till i reach the gravel road
once again haunted by the sound of my own feet
and the last words of mrs budris
"happy thanksgiving to you . . . young man"

Birnie

tonight thursday
another evening shift tomorrow
and the week'll be over
six of us slowly opening our lunchboxes
so tired
we look like wet moccasins
flung against a barn door

the silence grows like familiar cold nudging into bone
bill hanowski savours his sandwich
with slow small nibbles
us younger caretakers uncomfortable in this silent language
of the prairies
wait for the first story to save us
where hanowski's sad eyes will become a northern lake
when the sun finds a hole in clouds above it

finally all begins one story leads to another
till birnie remembers the best one
"i bought a swather once bill
onna them driven by a powertakeoff from the
tractor you know
i was wearin an ole paira pants
n my pant leg got caught in the powertakeoff
tore the pant leg right off
well i went home n gotta nuther paira pants
an ole pair
couldn take chances you know
well... lost another pant leg
n nearly the leg itself
the wife drove me to the hospital
when she brought me back she said
you crazy bugger you putta guard on that powertakeoff
before you kill yourself

then there was this woman back home in kendall
maiden name was *lang*
but er married name's *nosestad*
one day
her brother n er husband were diggin post holes inna pasture
she was wearin an ole denim jacket widda frayed sleeve
when she took lunch out to them
anyway before they knew what happened
she was spinnin round that drive shaft like wind
wrappin a blanket round a clothesline
they say er husband froze in the tractor seat
couldn move a finger
er brother ran up n grabbed a holda the drive shaft
thinkin he could stop it i guess
lost a hand clear at the wrist
the husband finally gotta hold ov imself
n shut the tractor off
took em both home n went for the doctor
they say er arm ad bin torn clean from the socket
wasn a drop a blood flowin
when the doctor arrived he pronounced er dead
n started fixin up the brother's hand
well . . . she opened er eyes n said
i am not dead
guess she musta bin in shock

anyway they rushed er to the hospital
n she's still livin today
in the wascana centre hospital
paralyzed from the neck down
they say she paints the most beautiful prairie scenes you
ever seen
water colour stuff you know
holds a paint brush in er mouth
every weekend they take er back home to kendall
yeah er husband went grey that year
lemme see . . . well there's nuthin in this room that grey

was another fulla once back home
nick stremick was his name
had a breakdown

n he forgot to shut the powertakeoff off
as he was gettin off the tractor
universal joint caught a hold ov is pants
tore em clean off his backside
funny part was
he never ad any shorts on
his wife caught im sneakin in the back door
just a belt on!"

birnie shifts his chair sideways
pulls up his right pant leg
to show us where the powertakeoff got him
a depression resembling a buffalo wallow
just above the ankle
"the other marks are where i stopped a few baseballs
wen i caught ball inna thirties
we couldn afford shinguards in those days"

silence
birnie is 57 today
and into his second pack of rothmans
the third pack will be gone by 6 a.m. tomorrow morning
when he and his wife finish the other two cleaning jobs
at a store and city bar
tomorrow he may get four hours sleep
the bags under his eyes sag like a sack of flour
on a farmer's shoulder...
somewhere deep in birnie's mind
is the memory of water
from a 27 foot farm well north of the city
water he drank returning from the field on hot august days
water so cold it made the head hurt
and the thought grows
till all memory becomes a catcher's mitt
and dying prairie towns where he played baseball hang upsidedown
like a signal to the pitcher
one worktwisted finger for each name
montmartre
        vibank
                indian head
and in a watercolour blue sky

his whole life becomes a white ball
curving perfectly
right across home plate

"yup...it's a great world" says birnie
his favourite line shattering the silence
like a wellswung bat
something whispering in the language of dry grass
not yet
not yet

Betrayal of Earth

telling it like it never was
you will always lie
to tell another truth ending in
betrayal of earth

take old bill from nokomis
who farmed for 30 years on the southern edge
of last mountain
to move to regina where he's been an evening janitor
for 14 years

in his homestead dream back on the farm
he often became a great sandhill crane
floating on a high wind over pile o' bones

now home is bill's faithful polish wife
the *ukrainian co-op* on winnipeg street
where the finest *babushka* can be bought
the day before the anniversary
and dinner once a month at the *bokoria*
on victoria

home is bill's new orange lunchbox just like mine
he bought at the *army and navy*
three days after i arrived at work

home is the dream he snaps shut
inside his lunchbox at 7 p.m.
to work another 5 hours
till the drive back south on winnipeg
to see the late movie on tv with his wife

bill can spraybuff tiles better than anyone
on this earth
and he is proud humming the old slavic songs
during his daily work

The Graveyard

the industrial vacuum cleaner
faithfully it follows me and follows me
through *family farm improvement*
follows me through *probation* offices
and *welfare* waiting rooms
it is a good machine only doing its job
helping me out

i wonder if it sometimes senses my rage
and utter futility
my desire to silence its ceaseless scream
with this heavy handle
pummelling it into a crumpled aluminum death
but then it knows
that i know that
such an incident two weeks before christmas
could only end with me being
signed away with a christmas turkey
to the weyburn clinic for the insane
we both know the probation officers
know me too well

nightly it sings
"the poem comes and goes
comes and goes
the poem never gets written
and lovely is our
three acre floor"

Poem Written to Old Friends at Christmas Time

these are but shadows
of things that have been
                               A Christmas Carol

mauve clouds beyond
brick warehouses illuminated light red
by the day's late last sun
and the whole wall text across winnipeg street reads

      HIDES   FURS
     FRANK MASSIN
      TANNING CO.

christmas eve
a janitor on the late shift i lock doors
while a beautiful young welfare worker
escorts three staggering cree to the last door still open
they exchange the season's best
as she wishes them a good and safe journey to lac la ronge
to see the newborn son of one of the wives

i wait
knuckling my ring of keys
wishing i were one of the travellers
instead of a cigarette butt in an ashtray
to all these office workers whose hellos are as rare
as a hooker's kiss

locking the last door and a final thought...
so many past things shut from the memory
so many friends
come and gone...

i turn to memories of those who remain as shadows
along margins of meaning in friendship
and something from the past present or even future
speaks in a halfwhisper
"you have all changed and grown
choosing different lives in distant cities"
a lonely thought...
i'm still here and what has not changed is
my inability to change
move on
though i'm forever moving on

we live our own lives
becoming a shadow of what we used to be
to rediscover ourselves some rare evening over beer
or a day's fishing
in high mountains or northern lakes

our stories grow fewer
as the need to retell them lessens
new friends become a promise of home
that crumbles
like a bridge crossing the river
beyond our aging eyes

tomorrow i'll be boarding a bus bound for a southern prairie town
will be carrying two presents
one for my failing father
and another for my mother
who no longer live with one another
though they are still where it all began and ended
when i fled to find you all in your distant cities
more remote than the stars of this holy night

Letter to Harold Ogle

harold... what ever happened to you?
whenever i'm home in wood mountain
they often ask
"you ever heard or seen anything of buzz?"
buzz... who the hell ever nicknamed you
that silly american navy pilots' name
it was always
"*buzz* and *rocks*" you and that police dog
you returned with the last few times

harold you were always so full of stories:
hitchhiking on $2 from wood mountain to squaw valley
your beautiful lost women
sending love letters thick as pulp hollywood magazines
summers in the mountains
you wrangler trailguide seasonal parks warden the whole gambit
christ knows how many bear stories you told me
the great drama... you and rocks
surviving every time
and you were so full of homespun philosophy
or you would quote that silly kipling poem
"if you can walk with counts and kings..."
and it took eternity before i could add
"yes... you will be a man
the *only* one"
yeah harold you could wax on for hours
and you were strange strange medicine
halfwhite halfindian
yammering ceaselessly of your friend hemingway
and all those sun valley and ketchem winters
where he taught you how to mix drinks properly
and you always dreamed of some wayout novel
you would someday write
just like kerouac's *on the road*...

but what ever happened to you man
after that last summer in the rockies
where i still sometimes search for your myth
where did you disappear to
after you fell into the bow river
breaking your arm for the second year in a row
because you hadn't cinched your saddle properly?
you were so certain the place was jinxed
and you cursed that wealthy stable owner
who you believed had it in for you

i don't know what it is and can't understand it
but in recent years now harold
i go back like you again and again to wood mountain
every spring and fall for a few weeks
hoping more and more to finally stay someday
when you were just dying to leave one day
and never return again
just as you've done
i still have no car
and often find myself hitchhiking
even though i know i'm getting too old for this folly
always trying to understand
what it was you were looking for
and it all seems as crazy as a meadow lark
singing in the middle of a flash blizzard that one spring
by the edge of the air base outside moose jaw
sometimes on quiet evenings in wood mountain harold
i can still hear you whistling your way
down late night streets
that are even more desolate now
tunes like
"just walking in the rain...
well i never felt more like singin the blues..."
what the hell ever the tune was
harold... what was it
you were running away from?
what is it i keep returning to?

sometimes i run into your mother at the co-op store in assiniboia
and no longer ask her about you
or if she's heard from you

knowing it gives her too much pain
often she sneaks up behind me and embraces me
her way of saying "guess who..."
but her smooth dark brown hands
and that turquoise and silver ring
you once found
while you hitched near some arizona reserve
always gives her away... harold
i've secretly named her
"the lovely ageing one who keeps memory at bay
and yearly embraces me like a wind
while waiting for the return of her son
some wood mountain spring"
yes harold... what ever happened to you
fleeing so perfectly from your indian ancestry?
did you finally like your grandfather the english lord
ride dressed in your warden's uniform
to some high mountain lookout point
and glimpse still another
new parking lot by the cpr hotel in lake louise
and decide to emigrate to england
for the ultimate solution:
your simple blonde sweetheart
from the bentley lineage
and a complete english tradition
that would pacify your yearnings for home

2 p.s.

i got a room here at the park hotel last night
harold... wasn't this the place where you worked
a porter that winter of 53?
you remember that following spring
how one sunday you drove down to wood mountain
with your girlfriend that lovely young tickettaker
from the moose jaw animal park?
well this summer in the mountains
i was lovers with an eastern lady
who looked exactly like her

oh yeah... do you remember that beautiful woman
from the reserve
the one who always sang that song saturday afternoons
on CHAB in moose jaw
remember that song?
"if teardrops were pennies
and heartaches were gold
i'd have all the money..."
well they say she grew old on river street
and as the old line goes
she went west... a few years ago

you know harold
a friend of ours
claims to have read an AP story from new york
something about a brawl in a harlem bar
and a man stabbed 40 times
the victim's description fitting you harold
is it true... that you actually
went west too?

At the St Victor Petroglyph Site

for eli mandel

those petroglyphs
along the road to wood mountain
they are the lost language of a people who were whole
knowing the transient meaning of home
and what is
prairie...

and a man lost deep in his summer's urban reverie
is a ghost already there again
searching for answers
something both fur and claw moving back
or ahead into time
before art spirit and hunter became chapters
in a white man's book
and the homeless ghost does not know
if it is the dry autumn grass speaking
what crumpled leaves speak
in the vernacular of fissured stone
...or if it is the distant jewish relative
enduring far beyond the abandoned
coalmines
and so many sunken places

you're just suffering wilderness withdrawal
too many mountain summers
manitou...you white men
obsessed with crosseyed shamans and
embarkations of our vanished young
journeying into adulthood all
chronicled in the rare stones of these hills
...or so you say
sometimes i wonder who
are the indians

a man moving in an urban dream
to reply
"say what you please
...i speak only of the pain
and loss i know
the rest i leave to the archaeologists
and you
whoever you are
your silent
entombed wisdom
that yields no peace..."

2

bear paw
        sun
butterfly
        engraved on the edge
of fissured stone

north
and far below
the shallow lake mirrors the sun's glare
and clouds
that know no country
or line of demarcation

3

arriving on this high hill
above the pain
of your understanding
being what you are
no more
no less
than the engraved sun
that could fit inside
the bear's paw
seeming so human

this
and what we bring with us
... the changed proportions
all things being equal in the signature
of the human spirit
a shadow
briefly etched across stone
before leaving

Returning

home again
to walk the abandoned
cpr y on the village edge
and notice how the rumanian church
has grown older
the two crosses no longer perfectly vertical
the way vizena placed them
on the steeples

the vague meaning of home
you carry within you
moving back and forth
across this vast country

the swift startling flight
of two nesting partridges
tracing the edge
of all you know   all
you dream